W9-BIM-074

A PASSAGE THROUGH GRIEF

A Recovery Guide

A PASSAGE THROUGH GRIEF

A Recovery Guide

BARBARA BAUMGARDNER

BROADMAN
& HOLMAN
PUBLISHERS

Nashville, Tennessee

© 1997, 2002
by Barbara Baumgardner
All rights reserved
Printed in the United States of America

0-8054-2628-0

Published by Broadman & Holman Publishers
Nashville, Tennessee

Hard cover edition published by Broadman & Holman
in 1997 is now out of print. (0-8054-6072-1)

All Scripture quotations are from the Holy Bible,
New International Version, © 1973, 1978, 1984
by International Bible Society.

4 5 6 7 8 9 10 06 05 04

In loving memory of those special people who enrolled me in the school of grief: You taught me how to grow.

Husband Dick

Only eighteen when we married. Thank you for three spirited, sensational daughters and thirty-one incredible years to play the role of wife.

Granddaughter Wendy

Never more beautiful than at her last prom. You were in full bloom at seventeen—so young to be plucked away. We miss you, Honey. My earring box misses you too.

Dad Mize

A tough teacher, a fair father, and a good provider. You taught me honesty, good morals, and to step out into life unafraid to pursue my goals and dreams.

Hospice of Bend

My sincere "thanks" to the staff who encouraged me as I developed this journaling program and then trusted me to teach and perfect it with grieving survivors. A special round of applause for all those who attended my grief journaling classes and wrote about your broken hearts and shattered dreams. You were the wind beneath my wings.

Most of all, my gratitude is to a holy God who faithfully walked beside me through the valley of mourning, encouraged me in the deep, dry wells of my writing, and squeezed my hand when I caught my first glimpse of Hope. Thank You for showing me Your plan for life after bereavement. I love You.

Contents

Introduction

Dear Friend:

A death has occurred, and you have been changed. Whether your loved one died slowly from the effects of a disease or a catastrophic event like a school shooting, a terrorist attack or a plane crash, your life will never be the same. That day of death left you filled with shock, grief, and perhaps anger and fear—a dark sorrow beyond anything you ever thought you could survive. But you did survive, and now you search for an end to your pain. I want to take your hand and walk with you on that journey.

You will find the stories in this book written by survivors of many kinds of losses. Along our journey we, too, stumbled and staggered, fell down, bounced off the walls, and discovered bruises in places we didn't even know we'd bumped. People held out a hand, gave a hug, encouraged, and offered comfort. We needed that, but most of all we needed *Hope*.

On my own journey through the valley of the shadow of death, *Hope* emerged when I found that God, whom I feared had forgotten me, was there all the time. I discovered He truly was in the dark places of my pain. He came to me as I wrote words in my journal—pain-coated words about my loss and my sorrow.

I pray that you'll find Him, too, in the deep, dark crevices of your grief and that your journey through this book will end in *Hope* and *Healing*.

Please accept my sympathy on the loss of your loved one. It is important to me that you know my thoughts and prayers are with you.

BARBARA BAUMGARDNER

Putting Grief into Words

Grief is not a problem to be cured.
It is simply a statement
that you have loved someone.

A DEATH HAS OCCURRED

A death has occurred
and everything is changed
by this event.
We are painfully aware
that life
can never be the same again,
that yesterday is over,
that relationships once rich
have ended.
But there is another way
to look upon this truth.
If life went on the same
without the presence of
the one who has died,
we could only conclude
that the life we here remember
made no contribution,
filled no space,
meant nothing.
The fact that this individual
left behind a place
that cannot be filled
is a high tribute
to this individual.
Life can be the same
after a trinket
has been lost,
but never after
the loss of a treasure.

PAUL IRION[1]

Understanding the Process of Journaling

If some aspects of your loved one's death are too difficult to talk about, or if you seem to be stuck at some point in your grief work, you may find that the act of writing out your thoughts will help you clarify and come to grips with them.

This process is called "journaling." Hopefully, this book will become your road map and guide into the concept of journaling your way through sorrow. Journaling can be an important step toward maintaining good mental health during bereavement, especially in the dark of the night when struggles with grief seem to intensify and sleep eludes you. Writing is particularly useful for those of you who didn't get to say "good-bye."

You can write anytime you need to talk. It is a safe way to discharge anger that might otherwise be directed toward someone still living.

Journaling can help diminish any guilt and be a more comfortable way to unload sorrow you are not willing to share with another human being.

Perhaps one of the most compelling reasons of all to write is that it preserves the memories, and that can be a very special "love gift" to family and friends. Writing can be your labor of love.

There is no time limit or expectation for completing your journal. No one will judge you or your writing abilities as each person will contribute in his or her own unique way. If you are participating in a grief journaling support group, hopefully you will become comfortable with sharing and reading aloud. You should feel safe with the other members of your group.

If you are taking your journey through this book alone, don't hurry. Pause as needed to reflect and heal amidst the recording of your special memories. I hope you'll find journaling is a pleasant journey that never ends as paper and pencil become your companion and friend.

Determine to allow your grief to flow freely onto the paper. Once written, it will be more easily set free. Anticipate the day when you will not want to hold onto your sorrows but instead release them. Then joy and peace can take up residency in your once fragmented life.[2]

Beginning

Take a few moments to be still before God. Listen as He reminds you that you are not alone in your grief. Psalm 46:1 says, "God is our refuge and strength, an ever-present help in trouble." You can count on that.

Don't be embarrassed if emotions and tears find their way to the surface. They are part of the healing process.

Think about your loss and the hole left in your life by the person who died. Name that relationship: your child, wife or husband, a parent, sibling, or friend. Say his or her name aloud.

This is not the time to review the reactions of other people or to dwell upon details such as the deceased's medications or complications. This is a time to examine your own self and your relationship with the deceased.

- How long did you know the spouse, parent, child, sibling, or friend?
- Was the death sudden or expected?
- How are you coping with the loss, and what help are you getting?
- What are your expectations from these journaling sessions?

If you are in a group setting, use the following lines to write down the names of others in your group, noting the nature of their loss and other information you may want to remember about them. Use a separate piece of paper if needed.

If you are soloing through this journal, use the space to write the answers to the above questions. Describe who you are now that this loss has occurred. How has it changed you?

_____

_____

_____

_____

You grieve differently from other people—not so differently that you cannot find fellowship in suffering with them, yet so differently that no one else's grief is exactly like your own.

WAYNE E. OATES[3]

Sometimes, we don't understand exactly how we feel until we see what we think on paper. To begin your journaling, pick up your pencil. Think about an experience (happy or unpleasant), you had with the one who had died. Don't worry about form or punctuation or spelling. Begin by making some brief notes in the form of an outline and then go back and fill in the details. Feel free to rewrite, cross out, erase, or fill in. This outline will help you to begin.

An incident to remember:

_____

_____

_____

Describe the day:

_____

_____

_____

_____

The setting:

_____

_____

_____

_____

The sounds:

_____

_____

_____

_____

The smells:

_____

_____

_____

_____

The prevailing emotions:

_____

_____

_____

_____

The people involved:

_____

_____

_____

_____

Now using the outline, tell your whole story. Add pages if needed. This writing is best done at home when you are all alone, enabling your emotions to flow freely without the distraction of sympathy or audience.

Date:_____

_____

_____

_____

_____

_____

_____

In every winter's heart,
there is a quivering spring,
and behind the veil of each night
there is a smiling dawn.
                    KAHLIL GIBRAN[4]

Meeting Other Journalists

Thelda Bevens is a former participant in a grief journaling group at the Hospice of Bend, Oregon.

Along with others, Thelda found hope and healing from writing about the death of her loved one.

"The Dance" and most of the stories to follow have been contributed by people (both named and unnamed) who journaled their way to recovery.

Some of their writing has undergone minor editing but only to shorten it for use here.

I am grateful to each donor for the gift of these excerpts from their journals. To each, I extend my sincere "thank you."

Thelda had been widowed for only six weeks when she attended her first session of a journaling group. When asked to write about a memory, she chose a happy one and called it "The Dance."

> Dar and I loved to dance. It was probably the first thing we did together, long before we knew we would share our lives.
>
> We grew up in a small Oregon mountain community where dances were held almost every Saturday night, sometimes in the school gym, sometimes at the Grange Hall, sometimes at the home of Nelson Nye. Nelson and his family loved music and dancing so much that they added a special room to their house large enough to accommodate at least three sets of square dancers. Once a month or more, they invited the entire community to a dance. Nelson played the fiddle and his daughter, Hope, played the piano while the rest of us danced.

In those days, the entire family went together—including the grandparents, the farmers and loggers, the school teachers and store owner. We danced to songs such as "Golden Slippers" and "Red Wing," side-by-side with contemporary ones like "Red Sails in the Sunset" and "It's a Sin to Tell a Lie."

Smaller children always had a place to sleep among the coats, close at hand, when they tired. It was a family affair, one of the few entertainments in a small mountain town climbing slowly out of the Great Depression.

Dar was 17 and I was 12 when we first danced. He was one of the best dancers on the floor and so was I. We always jitterbugged. No slow dancing for us, nothing remotely romantic. Our fathers would stand along the wall and watch, smoking their cigarettes. They weren't friends. They didn't talk to each other, not even a casual conversation. Both good dancers themselves, they were proud of their kids. Every once in a while, Dar's dad would smile a little, shake his head and say, to no one in particular, but so my dad could hear, "Boy, my kid can sure dance."

My dad never blinked an eye, acted like he'd never heard. But a while later he would say, to no one in particular, "That girl of mine can sure dance." And being of the old school, they never told us we were that good or had stirred that tiny bit of boastful rivalry along the wall.

Our dancing together stopped for five years while Dar was in the South Pacific in World War II. During those five years, I grew up. When we met again, Dar was 22 and I was almost 18. We began to date—and dance again.

This time it was for ourselves—finding our moves, our turns, our rhythms—adjusting, anticipating, enjoying. We were as good together as we remembered, and this time we added slow dancing to our repertoire.

For us, the metaphor fits. Life is a dance, a movement of rhythms, directions, stumbles, missteps, at times slow and precise, or fast and wild and joyous. We did all the steps.

We made our moves. We laughed and cried and did our dance.

Two nights before Dar died, the family was with us as they had been for several days—two sons and their wives and four of our eight grandchildren. We all ate dinner together and Dar sat with us. He hadn't been able to eat for several weeks, but he enjoyed it all—told jokes, kidded the boys about their cribbage playing, played with two-year-old Jacob.

Afterward, while the girls were cleaning up the kitchen, I put on a Nat King Cole tape, "Unforgettable." Dar took me in his arms, weak as he was, and we danced.

We held each other and danced and smiled. No tears for us. We were doing what we had loved to do for over fifty years, and if fate had so ordained, would have gone on doing for fifty more. It was our last dance—forever unforgettable. I wouldn't have missed it for the world.

Thelda Bevens[5]

The measure of a life after all,
is not its duration, but its donation.
PETER MARSHALL[6]

Perhaps as you read Thelda's story, your own emotions or memories began to surface. Can you describe them? Sometimes survivors feel anger or relief, or even abandonment. Make some notes to describe your feelings. Then, when you are ready to write, use your notes as suggested topics.

Thoughts, Memories, and Emotions!

_____

_____

_____

_____

_____

_____

_____

_____

_____

_____

_____

_____

_____

Maybe you'd prefer to write a very short story. The important thing is that you write something.

Maryal Beauvais expressed her feelings this way:

Tonight I wear my Auntie Mildred's nightgown and robe that she left behind in the guest room, all that is left from the many stays with us while she endured another chemo treatment, another radiation treatment.

I won't have to help her through another ordeal of cancer treatments. We will not watch another movie together or play pinochle. She will not help me through another recipe, or bring insight to a troubled relationship for me, or hem another pair of pants, or share the beauty of nature with me again.

Tonight I cry and feel sad and alone. Tonight I will wear her nightgown and feel close.[7]

Men and Grief

Most people know that the shortest verse in the Bible is "Jesus wept" (John 11:35). Yet many men find it difficult to emulate Jesus in this act of mourning. They've been taught the "be strong" ethic, to "be a man and don't cry." What an injustice to humanity!

Carol Staudacher, in her book *Men and Grief*, discloses how a woman is usually more communicative about her loss, and therefore is more likely to seek support and attend grief recovery sessions. A man, on the other hand, may feel highly private about his grief and fearful that he may not be doing it right. Finding the time to mourn is often difficult.

It is not uncommon for men to use aggression, anger, and violence as grief substitutes. It is their way of masking fear and insecurity. Most men simply don't know how to grieve the loss of someone they love.

Men are less likely to attempt to "journal" their grief, believing they can "take control" of this as they are accustomed to doing with other things. Fear of disclosing intimate information causes them to "stuff" their feelings, unaware of the negative consequences which may appear in the months and years to come. So if you are a man working through this journaling program, let me say, "Good for you!" You have taken a valuable step toward healing. You will never regret it.

Journaling is the axe that chips away the pain, but you must grab the handle in both hands. Whether you are taking this journaling journey alone or with a group, I hope you'll resolve to *allow* the natural and normal grief responses to happen:

15

- Feel the mood changes.
- Cry at unexpected times.
- Talk with people when you need to.
- Don't put a lid on your pain; let it out.
- Forget about becoming your "old self" again. Expect change.
- Allow yourself sufficient time to let the grieving take its unconstrained course, and insist that others allow you this time as well.
- Don't be in a hurry to replace the person who died with another hoping their presence will ease your sorrow. When you get well, you may find they were only a bandage for your pain.
- Allow God to renew your faith. There is no thought God doesn't know and no act He doesn't see. There's never a cry He doesn't hear nor a heart He can't mend.

When Benjamin Franklin concluded a stirring speech on the guarantees of the Constitution, a heckler shouted, "Aw, them words don't mean nothin' at all. Where's all the happiness you say it guarantees us?"

Franklin smiled and replied, "My friend, the Constitution only guarantees the American people the right to pursue happiness; you have to catch it yourself."

So it is with this journaling program. You have in your hands a book of guidelines for healing, but you have to "catch it" yourself. Rolling away the stone in front of your own sepulchre is no easy task; it takes choosing. I urge you to place your shoulder against the rock.

The waste of life lies in the love we have not given, the powers we have not used, the selfish prudence which will risk nothing and which, shirking pain, misses happiness as well.[8]

Elie Bourque was one of those men who found comfort in journaling. He said he felt a compelling drive to write. You see, Elie and Ginny were high school sweethearts. They celebrated their fiftieth wedding anniversary the year before Ginny died. Elie wrote:

Throughout the entire five-week period of loving and caring for and attending to Ginny and until she accepted our Lord's embrace, I had a compelling drive to sit down at my new computer and record my thoughts, memories, and emotions. Needless to say, I had many sleepless nights. This allowed me to think about and digest what was happening to all of us.

I never realized how painful, heavy, yet empty the heart can be. Now I know what a broken heart is. I feel very alone and that half of me has left this world. I guess when two people love each other and are as close to one another as we were and enjoy so many of the same things as we did, it is very difficult when one leaves.

When the oncologist explained the seriousness of Ginny's condition, calling it the "most devastating type of cancer," I remember thinking, *I do not want to hear this.* I was hoping for more encouraging words.

I was really proud of her courage to ask, "How long do I have?" She was a strong, realistic, and gutsy woman. I was still in shock and for the most part speechless. I wanted to know but didn't want to know . . . .

We had to make these few precious weeks count.[9]

Are you identifying with Maryal or Elie? If so, how? Write about that or perhaps about how your situation is different.

Title: _____

Date _____

_____

_____

_____

_____

_____

_____

_____

_____

_____

Bits and Pieces from Other Journalers

I'm feeling much better this week mostly because of the writing/journaling group: the warmth, the encouragement, the intelligence, the listening—sharing deep personal feelings and experiences. Ellen and packing the boxes, Pat and her strong faith, Bobbie with a new bed and yet feeling the presence of her husband, Maryal wondering how things could have been different, and Barbara encouraging us and letting us express our pain, listening, making us feel OK about our feelings and our writing.

THELDA BEVENS[10]

I have worn some clothing of Bob's like the Patagonia jacket and pull-on-pants but felt nothing except thankfully warm on a cold day. I sense that there must be something wrong with my feeling so severed. Is the deep wound still oozing my life's flow so that I am not capable of anything else right now? I hear the words again—"it takes time." But surely there must be more than just time to bring about healing.

SYBIL GIBSON[11]

At times I get so angry at what your illness put our family through. How it changed all our lives forever. You are gone and we are left here, still going over and over your illness and what happened. You left it behind with us to understand. I don't understand!

I want you to tell me what was on your mind when you took your life. Were you hating me? Was the timing intentionally meant to hurt me? My wedding and your funeral in the same week! I feel mad, then guilty, then sad. Yet, through your sickness, I have learned sensitivity to all people. I have learned not to judge people by their looks, but to listen to their hearts. You have taken me to another level in life, to a deeper layer of emotion. I can feel more pain at times but I also feel more love and happiness. Through you, I am a different person, a better person.

SUZANNE MCELROY[12]

I hate it when I know bad days are coming and I can't do anything to head it off. I walk around with my eyes watering all of the time. I tell myself it's allergies, but in the middle of the night, I know it's tears. I am weary of being victorious over death. Let the old codger have his day of glory. This is a very difficult time for Dad. He walks around weeping, as I do. Darn those allergies!

MARYAL BEAUVAIS[13]

Some Things I'm Thinking, Feeling, Wishing, Hoping, Doing:

Date: _____

_____

_____

_____

_____

_____

_____

_____

_____

_____

_____

_____

Stages of Grief

Congratulations!

It has taken a lot of courage for you to be willing to move on to session 2. Let me reassure you, it will become easier each time. So don't let your apprehension get in your way of participating and benefiting from this journal. If you feel pain as you attempt this writing, it's because your pain is being released. You are not stuffing it but setting it free!

When the bereaved are so involved in their pain and loss, they sometimes forget that God wants to be a source of comfort. They find it difficult to maintain fellowship with Him but even at those times when your deep sadness turns to despair, a verse from God's Word can bring hope.

> "Blessed are those who mourn for they will be comforted."
>
> MATTHEW 5:4

> "For the Lord comforts his people and will have compassion on his afflicted ones."
>
> ISAIAH 49:13B

When you write in your journal, there are no right or wrong topics, no right or wrong emotions, no right or wrong way to record your journey through the grief process. C. S. Lewis, in keeping his journal, discovered that "grief is not a state, but a process, and that is the value of putting thoughts on paper—one can look back and see that progress is being made."[1]

What are the changes that have taken place in your life since the day your loved one died? Are you no longer married or do you no longer have a mother? Do you now live alone for the first time in your life? On the following lines make a list or write a story about those changes.

Date: _____

_____

_____

_____

_____

_____

_____

_____

_____

_____

Ten Stages of Grief

1. We are in a state of shock. When sorrow is overwhelming, we are sometimes temporarily anesthetized because it keeps us from having to face the grim reality all at once. Shock is a temporary escape from reality. Shock makes it difficult to make decisions.

2. We express emotion. Emotional release comes at about the time it begins to dawn upon us how dreadful this loss is. Often, without warning, emotional release begins to be expressed. We ought to express the grief we feel. Scripture shows clearly that when great calamities came to the hardy men of faith, they wept bitterly; their "tears were with them all night long" (1 Sam. 30:4).

3. We feel depressed and very lonely. Eventually there comes a feeling of utter depression and isolation. It is as if God is no longer in His heaven, as if God does not care. Such depression is a normal part of good, healthy grief, and it will pass.

"My tears have been my food day and night, while men say to me all day long, 'Where is your God?' I say to God my Rock, 'Why have you forgotten me?'" (Ps. 42:3, 9a)

4. We may experience physical symptoms of distress. Some people are ill because of unresolved grief. No amount of medicine will significantly change the need to work through the emotional problems of unresolved grief.

"Be merciful to me, O LORD, for I am in distress; my eyes grow weak from sorrow, my soul and my body with grief." (Ps. 31:9)

5. We may become panicky. We can think of nothing but the loss, even when we try to get our mind off the subject. We cannot concentrate and wonder what is wrong with us. Worry and fear that we are going through something wholly abnormal throws us into deeper despair. It is comforting to know that even panic is normal.

6. *We feel a sense of guilt about the loss.* Real or normal guilt is the guilt we feel about some of the things we did or did not do for the person when he or she was alive. Neurotic guilt is feeling guilty all out of proportion to our own real involvement in this particular problem. Praying, "Create in me a clean heart, O LORD, and renew a right spirit within me" (Ps. 51:10), can bring a remarkable sense of relief.

7. *We are filled with anger and resentment.* These feelings are normal for even the most devout person. However, we must admit to ourselves that we need to confess and ask God for strength to rise above it.

8. *We resist returning to life.* Something inside us keeps us from going back to our usual activities. This is often the desire to keep the memory of our tragedy alive. We become comfortable in our grief and fearful that everyone has forgotten our pain.

9. *Gradually hope comes through.* We become aware that we can smile or laugh again. There dawns a consciousness that others also have problems. While no two people are the same, most recipients of encouragement will begin to believe, "I can make it."

10. *We struggle to affirm reality.* When we go through any significant grief experience, we come out of it as different people. How we respond will make us either stronger people or weaker—either healthier in spirit or sicker. Many develop a deeper faith in God as a result of their grief experiences.[2]

It is important to keep nurturing one's faith. Like the athlete who must stay in training, the faithful are always in training for whatever may come at any time. It is also important to realize that life will never be the same again, but there is much in life that can be affirmed.

At the time of great loss, people who have a mature faith give evidence of an uncommon relationship with God. And they demonstrate an uncommon inner sense of strength and poise which grows out of the confidence that such a relationship with God can never be taken away from them. With that assurance they can face any earthly loss. They still have God on whom to rely. It makes an amazing difference in the quality of the grief experience.

> May my cry come before you, O Lord;
> give me understanding according to your word.
> May my supplication come before you;
> deliver me according to your promise.
>
> Psalm 119:169–70

The list of the "Stages of Grief" will help you understand some of your feelings. You may not go through all the stages. The order often varies, and some stages return again and again.

After reading the list, try to identify the stages you have already experienced. Write about the stage(s) you feel you are in now. What is helping you?

Remember, your writing is best done when you are alone at home, in your favorite chair, or in the stillness of the night when the family is sleeping.

Sometimes finding a quiet place in the park or sitting by a babbling brook might help you get in touch with your feelings.

STAGES OF GRIEF

Gifts to Give Yourself

The following list offers some gift ideas to give yourself during bereavement.

Time: Time to be alone and time with people who are willing to listen when you want to talk. Time to pray, time to cry, and time to remember.

Rest: Extra sleep, unhurried hot baths, naps.

Hope: Being with others who have "survived" the death ordeal may offer you proof that you can heal.

Goals: Make a list of goals for today and another one for this week. Unless necessary, don't plan far ahead right now.

Goodness: Take in a movie, eat a hot-fudge sundae with a friend, sit in a hot tub, or have a massage.

Permission to backslide: Old feelings of sadness, despair, or anger may return. This is normal and should not be considered failure. Accept it as a "bad day" and remember, "This, too, will pass."

A special friend: It is important that you not attempt to handle grief alone. At some time you need to share your responses to grief with a good friend or someone who can listen objectively. If you become concerned about your progress over a period of six to nine months, don't hesitate to get some professional counseling.

Be sure to date your journalings so that as your feelings and emotions change, you'll be able to document your progress.

Date: _____

Today my emotions are:

_____

_____

_____

_____

I wish I could feel:

_____

_____

_____

The weather-cock on the church spire, though made of iron, would soon be broken by the storm-wind if it . . . did not understand the noble art of turning to every wind.[3]

A Season of Suicide

"He took his own life," sounds like something he was entitled to do.

After all, it was his life to do with as he wished, wasn't it? Well, wasn't it?

When the news came, we numbly whispered impromptu answers as people insensitively questioned his motive. "Why hadn't he wanted to live? Was he depressed? A financial crisis—marriage problems?" And then the inevitable question, "Was I, his wife, to blame?"

Was I? Was I responsible for his life—and his death?

I tried to deny it happened. Bearing the grief of death was a full load by itself. I tried to avoid those friends who knew how he died. Their eyes questioned my bewildered existence.

As the survivor of my marriage, I hungered to know the truth, to ask the questions that could no longer be answered. Thus my journey through a season of self-examination became a tug-of-war between my life and his death.

It took time to recall circumstances that might have influenced my husband's self-destruction. As I dissected and analyzed each turbulent situation, I asked God to forgive me for my error or mishandling of the event, and then I forgave myself, knowing that there was no way I could change the past.

Painfully, tearfully, and slowly I examined our seasons together. When I finished, I was free and forgiven and no longer floundering in self-inflicted guilt.

No, I was not responsible for his life, and, therefore, was not responsible for his death. It was his choice to die—his way to escape from what he thought was an intolerable time.[5]

Suicide: Brings the survivors into the torment the deceased was trying to escape from.

Quoted from a journaling class participant

For of all sad words of tongue or pen,
The saddest are these: "It might have been"!
JOHN GREENLEAF WHITTIER[4]

Some of you are survivors of much publicized catastrophic tragedies such as a school shooting, an airplane crash, the Oklahoma City bombing, or the World Trade Center–Pentagon terrorist attacks. Does the circumstances of your loss set you apart from survivors of a loved one with cancer, heart attack, or old age? Explain:

_____

_____

Try to deal with any differences through writing and talking to other people in your group. Look up some Scripture about God's love: Isaiah 43:2; Matthew 5:4; 2 Corinthians 1:3–4; Psalm 119:50; Psalm 23:4; Hebrews 4:15–16. These verses make no distinction concerning who they are for but tell us to cast all our cares upon Him; for He cares for us—all of us. In Revelation 21:4 it says, "And God shall wipe away all tears from their eyes; and there shall be no more death, neither sorrow, nor crying, neither shall there be any more pain: for the former things have passed away." That's a promise from God! Hang on to it!

Some things I'm thinking, feeling, wishing, hoping, doing:

Date: _____

_____

_____

_____

_____

_____

_____

_____

_____

_____

_____

_____

Dearly Beloved

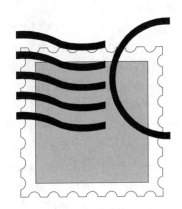

Letter Writing

You may find yourself becoming comfortable with (or even looking forward to) sharing what you have written with others. Sharing losses and celebrating victories pave the way to survival. However, there may be times you struggle to fight off an intense longing to talk to the one who died. It is helpful to write a letter to them. Pat Wester wrote this letter to her husband a year after his death:

> My Dearest Love:
>
> A year ago today, we had your funeral. It's hard to believe I have survived this year. It has been so hard.
>
> And yet I have learned so much. I've had to face my fears, no running away from them. Like the problem furnace—it's still acting up and overheating, and I hate it. Yet I have learned that God is faithful in every area. I've learned a lot about prayer and trust. I realize it is time to move on in this grief process. Hospice has been such a help. It reminds me that the time has come to leave the relationship we had and will never have again.
>
> In the past it seemed disloyal to stop grieving you . . . that my grief is the last tie I have with you. I took off my wedding rings yesterday. My hand feels naked. But I am not married now so I am experimenting with feeling single. I wear the beautiful opal ring you gave me on our seventeenth wedding anniversary. The tears flow as I write this.
>
> The holiday season is nearly here, but it seems so hollow and empty. I wish I could take a sleeping

pill and wake up on January 2. The children and grandchildren are coming so I must make an effort to celebrate, to decorate and cook. Those efforts will keep me busy and that will help. Good night, my love. I'll see you in eternity.

PAT[1]

In times of affliction we commonly meet with the sweetest experiences of the love of God.

JOHN BUNYAN[2]

I remember at one time, my need to talk to my husband overshadowed rationality. Deep inside, an urgency to share my thoughts, pain, questions, and needs smoldered and burned. Like Pat, I also wrote a letter:

Dear Dick:

Vikki shot a nice four-point buck on opening morning. You'd have been proud to see it. The orchard bloomed magnificently, and it looks like I'll have a good apple crop—probably because you pruned the trees back so much. I don't know what I'll do with all the apples, though.

I bought a new lawn mower—a big, really expensive one but I can't get it started any easier than the old one. Why aren't you here to fix that? Why? It's been such an awful time of adjusting, denying, pretending and hurting. Dick, I've missed you. Couldn't you have said, "good-bye"?[3]

Writing is an extension of who we are at the present moment.

Suppression leads to momentary relief and permanent pain. Feeling your experience leads to momentary pain and permanent relief.[4]

You, too, may find it helpful to clarify your thoughts about your loved one by recording your feelings in the form of a letter. Here are some ideas to get you started:

- What I miss most about you and our relationship
- What I wish I'd said or hadn't said
- What I've had the hardest time dealing with
- What I'd like to ask you
- Special ways I am keeping my memories of you alive

List some of your own ideas for topics:

_____

_____

_____

If you choose not to keep a letter, write it on a separate piece of paper instead of in your book. You may want to read it aloud at the grave site, read it to a friend, or to God. Sometimes people tear their letters into tiny pieces and let the wind carry them high into the sky.

A special love letter to the deceased can be re-read by candlelight, then ignited on the candle flame as you say good-bye, not to the *memory* but to the *person*.

For the letters you want to write and keep, use the following pages.

Date: _____

Dear _____

_____

_____

_____

_____

_____

_____

_____

_____

_____

_____

_____

_____

_____

Date: _____

Dear _____

_____

_____

_____

_____

_____

_____

_____

_____

_____

_____

_____

_____

_____

_____

Some feelings seem more difficult to write about than others. It takes making a decision, believing there is benefit in doing so. Here is the decision Ellen Rollins made following her teenage daughter's suicide.

Dear Kathy:

I sit in your newly cleaned room (you wouldn't recognize it!) and try to get in touch with you and with how I feel. I can't think or feel or write.

I took your Mickey Mouse sheets off your bed and the stuff down from the walls. I went through your drawers and boxes and read all the notes I found. I threw away your garbage, your half-eaten rabbit from last Easter, your gum wrappers. I poured out the beer I found in your sweaters. I gave away most of your clothes, your shoes that waited so long for you to come and wear them.

My heart has been waiting for you to come back too. My head has known for some time now that you are physically gone from my life, but my heart still loves you as a living part of my life. My arms still yearn to reach out to hold you safe.

I struggle with the knowledge that you did the only thing you saw you could do—I still want to send you the hope of other options—through your pain and mine.

I want to see other options for me than to clean your room, pack your life in boxes for the closet, and go on into my life without you.

I do see other options: I could follow your lead. I could remain here, crying in your room. I could stuff the feelings of your death and pretend to be OK.

But Kathy, I choose to live!

I choose the option I would want for you because I want life. I want to have the feelings and thoughts and nightmares I have over you because in doing that I set myself free!

I set myself free to go out into this day and feel the sun, see the spring flowers and to truly live. It is a gift I give myself. I wish you could have found that gift in your life.

With all my love, Mom[5]

His Part, Our Part

I believe the Lord often asks us to do our part before He will do His part. The story of the blind man in John 9:1–11 is a good example of that. The man had been blind since birth and longed to see as others could. When the disciples questioned his blindness, Jesus did a strange thing. He knelt down and spit in the dirt, making a paste of mud with his saliva. After applying the mud to the eyes of the blind man, he instructed him to go to the pool of Siloam and wash the mud off. When the man did his part, Jesus completed the miracle and the man received his sight.

To begin the healing process in our lives, our part is to ask. However, we must remember that there may be something Jesus will require of us before our healing can be completed. We have been blinded by death and grief, making it difficult to move on. Without the will to get past bereavement, many people stay stuck in their grief.

You are the only one who can set yourself free, as Ellen did. It was a gift she gave herself, and all her prayers for healing depended upon Ellen giving herself permission to heal.

When grief holds us in bondage, we can pray and pray; but until we are willing to accept the freedom that Christ can give, we will remain in bondage.

Are you feeling guilty about letting go of your grief? That is bondage.

Are you worried about what people will think if you stop grieving? That is bondage.

Are you fearful that sympathetic friends will abandon you if you get well? That is bondage.

Stop right now and ask God to reveal any bondage that holds you and keeps you from healing from the grief of your loss. You might want to pray a prayer similar to this:

> Dear God, You know my heart better than I do. I ask You to reveal to me any bondage that is blocking the way to my healing. I want to put this pain and grief behind me. Help me not to be concerned so much with what others will think of me, but show me how to live the life You have designed for me. Please forgive me for those times I chose to stay stuck looking inward instead of keeping my eyes on You. Thank You for the healing that I know is mine. Amen.

Be quiet and allow Him to speak to you. Take your time. As thoughts or decisions come into your mind, make notes so you won't forget them.

_____

_____

_____

_____

_____

_____

_____

_____

_____

Write a short note to God about an attitude or fear that may be blocking your healing. Be honest.

Dear God:

_____

_____

_____

_____

_____

You may also want to write a letter to God to tell Him about your disappointments, anger, loneliness, and sorrow. And tell Him how you have or have not felt comforted by Him.

This is a tough chapter. It is difficult enough to write to or about the one who died. Confronting God with your feelings is something you may not have ever considered. I hope you will discover as I did that God is big enough and wise enough to handle *anything* you want to talk to Him about. "For we do not have a high priest who is unable to sympathize with our weaknesses, but we have one who has been tempted in every way, just as we are—yet was without sin. Let us then approach the throne of grace with confidence, so that we may receive mercy and find grace to help us in our time of need." (Heb. 4:15–16)

If God feels distant and uncaring as is sometimes the case during bereavement, it is OK to tell Him exactly how you are feeling. Then ask Him to come close and make His presence known to you.

> He heals the brokenhearted and binds up their wounds.
>
> PSALM 147:3

> So do not fear, for I am with you; do not be dismayed, for I am your God. I will strengthen you and help you; I will uphold you with my righteous right hand.
>
> ISAIAH 41:10

While you are writing letters, have you considered writing some thank-you notes to the doctor, friends, the mortuary, or anyone else involved in this time of your life? Be sure to tell them you are working on your recovery.

List those you will write to:

_____

_____

_____

_____

_____

_____

Read these "Goals of Grief Recovery" aloud to another person if possible.

1. Admit that the person is really gone. Believe it; don't just say it.

2. Be willing to experience the pain. Pain is easy to get stuck in. It is a mistake to believe that if you go through the pain, it will get worse. When you permit the pain, it will mellow. Allow yourself to feel.

3. Adjust to the environment without the person. Say "good-bye for now" a little bit at a time.

4. Withdraw the emotional energy that you feel from the relationship and reinvest it in another cause or goal.

Some things I'm thinking, feeling, wishing, hoping, doing:

Date: _____

_____

_____

_____

_____

_____

_____

_____

_____

_____

_____

_____

_____

Creatively Speaking

In Touch with Emotions

Writing letters was probably difficult for you because the yearnings to actually deliver the messages brought pain. How did you deal with that?

_____

_____

_____

_____

_____

_____

_____

_____

_____

_____

As you read your letters again, take note of how you attempted to convey a thought or message to your deceased loved one. What emotions are present as you do this?

_____

_____

_____

_____

Did some of the letters help to resolve any unfinished business? Guilt? Loneliness? Anger? How? Describe a way you did or will resolve some of that.

_____

_____

_____

_____

What will you do with your letters?

_____

_____

_____

_____

Some people prefer to write poetry, and many find they do their best writing in moments of crisis.

GRIEF IS LIKE A RIVER

My grief is like a river—
I have to let it flow,
But I myself determine
Just where the banks will go.
Some days the current takes me
In waves of guilt and pain
But there are always quiet pools
Where I can rest again.
I crash on rocks of anger—
My faith seems faint indeed,
But there are other swimmers
Who know that what I need
Are loving hands to hold me
When the waters are too swift,
And someone kind to listen
When I just seem to drift.
Grief's river is a process
Of relinquishing the past,
By swimming in Hope's channels
I'll reach the shore at last.

CYNTHIA G. KELLEY[1]

For some people, it is difficult to write poetry. So, I took the rhythm from "Mary Had a Little Lamb" and came up with this:

Barbara had a aching heart
Where death left a gaping hole.
And everywhere that Barbara went,
The tears were sure to roll.
The tossing and turning of sleepless nights
Have filled my days with woe.
My broken heart cries out to ask,
"Why did you have to go?"

Now you try it. Pick a nursery rhyme and be creative:

_____

_____

_____

_____

_____

_____

_____

_____

For centuries men and women have found poetry to be food for the soul. Poetry has whispered healing words to mend a broken relationship and sung a melody to lull a baby to sleep. Writing poetry takes deep feeling and emotion. Poems often are birthed by grief.

After completing a grief journaling workshop, Sybil Gibson composed this poem.

LOSS OF MY BELOVED HUSBAND

I was like a bright kite, dancing so high
reaching for the sun in the windy sky,
when my supporting cord was severed.
In the turbulence, I shuddered and floundered
blown alone, around and around,
slipping away, dropping down and down.
Then stopping at last and finding myself
in the silence and desolation
of my sudden isolation.
Those closest to me were suffering too,
"what can we say?"—"what can we do?"
their own souls needing to soothe.
In my darkening cloud I yearned for light
and welcomed even a glimpse so slight
of God's provision for my plight.
I opened the Scriptures and sought in prayers,
gave thanks, asked blessings and yielded cares.
Yet grief swept over, stripping my soul bare.
God's people stepped in and lifted me up,
They too had drunk from a bitter cup.
They found the kite damaged but not destroyed.
And, bit by bit, they helped weave a new cord

by shining Christ's Light to help me to ford
this troublesome time. He still is my Lord.
Throughout this past year God's love and His Light
worked my dark places. A new cord is tied tight.
The kite has been healing and is ready for flight.
Come, Holy Spirit, blow and set me dancing.

SYBIL S. GIBSON[2]

Use this space to compose your own personal poetry.

_____

_____

_____

_____

_____

_____

_____

_____

_____

_____

Find a photo of your deceased loved one to paste on this page, and write a short description of him or her. Include the year and place the photo was taken.

_____

_____

_____

_____

_____

Why is this photo important?

_____

_____

_____

_____

_____

_____

_____

_____

_____

_____

_____

_____

_____

_____

There's an Elephant in the Room

There's an elephant in the room
It is large and squatting, so it is hard to get around it.
Yet we squeeze by with, "How are you?" and "I'm fine."
And a thousand other forms of trivial chatter.
We talk about the weather.
We talk about work.
We talk about everything else—except the elephant in the
*   room.*
There's an elephant in the room.
We all know it is there.
We are thinking about the elephant as we talk.
It is constantly on our minds.
For you see, it is a very big elephant.
But we do not talk about the elephant in the room.
Oh, please, say her name.
Oh, please, say "Barbara" again.
Oh, please, let's talk about the elephant in the room.
For if we talk about her death,
Perhaps we can talk about her life.
Can I say "Barbara" and not have you look away?
For if I cannot, you are leaving me
Alone . . . In a room . . .
With an elephant.

Terry Kittering[3]

58

Draw a sketch of how you are feeling right now. (Stick figures and childlike artwork would be fine.)

How did drawing make you feel?

_____

_____

_____

_____

Some things I'm thinking, feeling, wishing, hoping, doing:

Date: _____

_____

_____

_____

_____

_____

_____

_____

_____

_____

_____

_____

_____

_____

First Times

Who Am I?

Some people would rather withdraw to keep from hearing or using those difficult, descriptive words. Are words like *dead*, *death*, *widow*, and *widower* difficult for you to use in conversation?

Do you relate to the author of this poem?

> *Definition*
> *It means reading Hallmark cards*
> *"From both of us at Christmas"*
> *And knowing I am not*
> *Part of a "both" anymore.*
> *It means a hole in the middle*
> *Of a large and empty, queen-size bed,*
> *Rolling over to put my cold feet on*
> *A warm back and finding instead, a*
> *Cooling, hot-water bottle.*
> *It means hanging mistletoe*
> *And knowing he won't be there*
> *To catch and hold me under it.*
> *It means missing the smell of his*
> *After-shave, the wet towels on the*
> *Bathroom floor, and the cap always*
> *On the toothpaste, now.*
> *It means hearing Glenn Miller's*
> *"Moonlight Serenade," and he's not*
> *There to hold me close and*
> *Hum in my ear.*
> *It means eating dinner on a TV tray*
> *With Tom Brokaw or Dan Rather*

Instead of sharing his day
Over coffee by the fireplace.
It means being the "extra woman"
Instead of part of a fun couple.
Widow—it really means
Alone.

LINDA LORENZO[1]

On Being a Widow

Friends. Well-meaning friends. Well, of course we'll be in Yuma next winter. Do I even want to go back?

I am screaming inside. Where do I fit, now that I am single? Won't I be that proverbial fifth-wheel that people feel obligated to ask to the party, even though the party would get along just fine, even better, without me?

I am on the outside looking in, hearing their laughter, their sharing, their conversation about bike rides and $2 breakfasts and I am filled with resentment and anger.

Then this nasty sly thought slips in, fanning the flames of my anger. If I had died and my husband was the survivor, he would hook up the camper and head to Yuma at the first signs of winter. He'd play golf, accept dinner invitations, read, meet new people. He wouldn't feel like an intrusion into the couples' world.

It's different for men than women.

THELDA BEVENS[2]

Being in a "couples' world" is difficult for those who remember only being married. Describe how you think being widowed is different for men than it is for women.

_____

_____

_____

_____

_____

_____

Maybe you have been invited to a baby shower, and it hasn't been long since your child died. Describe your feelings.

_____

_____

_____

_____

_____

_____

When was the first time you were labeled by your loss (i.e. widow, widower)?

_____

_____

_____

When did you first use "that word" to refer to yourself?

_____

_____

_____

When did you first notice how much your responsibilities have changed?

_____

_____

_____

Me? Take the Trash Out?

Today, I took the trash can out to the street for the first time. Wayne and I had always taken the truck to the dump. Tomorrow, it will be picked up. This is just one more thing that has changed that Wayne is not a part of.[3]

MY FIRST MEMORIAL DAY

I look out the window to my garden. The bearded irises stand in cheerful two-purple celebration of spring. The pansies peek through the green to join the rites. The purple chive balls toss in the breeze happy to be here, alive on this rainy Memorial Day.

I'm glad I did not pick these flowers to take to some wet, far-distant cemetery to bear mute witness to my rememberings. When the sun comes out, I will take my green teacup filled with warm comfort out into the flowers and remember.[4]

Note Some of Your Firsts

First oil change in the car that was my responsibility:

_____

_____

_____

First time I did the laundry alone:

_____

_____

_____

First time to do the taxes alone:

_____

_____

_____

Other Firsts:

_____

_____

_____

_____

_____

_____

Nadine Smith says if she could do it all over, she'd do it differently. Or would she?

How many times have I said, "If I could do it over, I'd do it differently." If I knew then what I know now. Motherhood is not what it's cracked up to be. Being a mother brings so much stress, worry, pain, and sorrow. Now death has raised its ugly head and touched my child.

I love my children more than I love my own life. I really discovered this fact after the death of my firstborn son. I made the statement, "I would trade places with him in a heartbeat." I meant it. It would be so much better than this pain I'm drowning in. His life was just beginning; it's not natural to outlive your children.

The agony is compounded by the death of my dear daddy less than three months earlier. I feel guilty about the sporadic mourning of my father. He is on my mind always, yet somehow he gets lost in my grief for my son. Daddy was always there for me. Always ready to help, to give, to hold me, to pat me and say, "You'll be OK." I need him to say it now. My life's not OK.

I hunger for my son, Ronnie. I see him everywhere. I hear his truck drive into the driveway, and then reality hits me and I know it can't be him. My arms ache to hold him.

What I would give to see him flop down on our couch to watch TV or take a nap. To see his shy, kinda-smile and all his beautiful white teeth. Today I would even listen to his music. Although some of his choices weren't too bad, his rock and roll was horrendous. Oh, Ronnie, Mom misses you!

So, again I say, "I would live my life differently, never to be a mother, never to feel this much pain."

Had I chosen not to be a mother, I would have missed the pain, but also—I would have missed that miracle moment of birth. The first sight of my own flesh and bones in another form. Tiny, helpless, wrinkled, and so beautiful. They talk about love at first sight. It's real. I would have missed the first smile, the first tooth, the first step, that awful first day of school, the first job, the first car, the first girlfriend.

So many firsts, so many lasts. Thank You, Lord, I didn't miss even one.[5]

There will be many "firsts" and "lasts" that will make an impact on your life, possibly bringing increased sorrow—the first holiday without your loved one or another special day, like a birthday or the anniversary of the person's death. We will deal with those during the next session. In the space below, write about one or more of the other "firsts" and "lasts." How did you feel when it happened?

If you could do it over, how would you do it differently?

_____

_____

_____

_____

_____

_____

Stop and think about how far you've come in your recovery and in this workbook. Write about that.

_____

_____

_____

_____

_____

_____

_____

_____

_____

_____

Our Times Together

Last week, we talked in our writing session of how very much we each are strengthened and encouraged by these times together. The sparks of life that show in each of my new friends' writings are sure evidence that God is working in our lives even as we grieve.

I think it was Thelda who said that time together with this group is the high point in her week. And that is what it means to me too. Nothing else has even begun to help me by comparison.

Each of you is so willing to share your lives, your points of sorrow, your decisions for action (both mental and physical), and your glimpses of growth. Thank you for the gift of your transparent selves.

SYBIL GIBSON[6]

Dr. Alan D. Wolfelt is a contributing editor for *Bereavement* magazine. He defines "grieve" as the internal experience of thoughts and feelings that follow death. He defines "mourn" as the shared social response to loss.[7] He wrote, "Not until a secure, trusting relationship comes along will the survivor become capable of taking the grief that is inside and sharing it outside."[8]

If you've been taking the journey through this workbook alone, I want to encourage you to find someone who will listen to you talk about your loved one who died. No one should grieve alone. If you don't have a close friend or family, seek out a support group for the bereaved.

Call your church if you have one or look for a Bible-teaching church and talk to the pastor. The local Chamber of Commerce can give you information on the ministerial association in your community which can be helpful in finding a church.

Call the local hospice to see if they have a grief recovery program.

Write down the numbers here.

_____

_____

_____

_____

Some things I'm thinking, feeling, wishing, hoping, doing:

Date: _____

_____

_____

_____

_____

_____

_____

_____

_____

_____

_____

_____

Holidays and Special Days

Stepping-Stones

Have you any leftover feelings from the last session on "first times"? Any new discoveries? Any praises?

As long as you live, you will come face to face with "first-times." Calling upon God for renewed strength and an adventurer's heart will help. Some day you'll be able to thank Him for your new experiences and grow from them.

Holidays and special days can be unsettling experiences for at least the first year after the death of your loved one. Emotions may be more intense as those meaningful days approach; however, these are not setbacks. They are just the stumbling blocks in the dark tunnel of grief. Knowing they are there can help you to turn them into stepping-stones.

THE STEPPING-STONE PRAYER

I do not ask to walk smooth paths
Nor bear an easy load.
I pray for strength and fortitude
To climb the rock-strewn road.
Give me such courage I can scale
The hardest peaks alone,
And transform every stumbling block
Into a stepping-stone.

GAIL BROOK BURKET[1]

Think about a favorite part of the holidays enjoyed by the one who died. I remember my dad making divinity candy on Christmas Eve while we kids played Monopoly. We thought we couldn't wait until the sweet, creamy confection cooled enough for that first taste. Sometimes I got to clean out the bowl.

I think I've never tasted divinity like Dad made—I think it had something to do with the way he beat it with a wooden spoon while Mom poured the stream of hot syrup into the egg whites.

I wish I would have learned his secret before he died.

As you think about holidays past, make some notes here for the writing you will do when you are alone and quiet.

He or she enjoyed:

_____

_____

_____

You may find yourself writing more notes and lists as Thanksgiving and Christmas approach. Dealing with your loss is difficult enough without having to think about the holidays. However, most bereaved people will admit that anticipating the sadness of the day is worse than the actual day when it comes.

Make some notes here of things you want to write about, perhaps at a more convenient time.

I want to remember to write about

_____

_____

_____

When faced with a holiday or other special day, ask God to direct how you spend it and to bring someone to help make it easier. He knows your heart, your pain, and your need for emotional strength. Even difficult days will pass. Someday, we can know the truth of Revelation 21:4: "He will wipe every tear from their eyes. There will be no more death or mourning or crying or pain, for the old order of things has passed away."

This Too Will Pass Away

If I can endure for this minute
Whatever is happening to me,
No matter how heavy my heart is
Or how "dark" the moment may be—
If I can but keep on believing
What I know in my heart to be true,
That "darkness will fade with the morning"
And that THIS WILL PASS AWAY, TOO—
Then nothing can ever disturb me
Or fill me with uncertain fear,
For as sure as NIGHT BRINGS THE DAWNING
"MY MORNING" is bound to appear.

Helen Steiner Rice[2]

Surviving Holidays and Anniversaries

Holidays and anniversaries are very difficult for the person in grief. These are days of special remembrance and are often filled with bittersweet memories. The most difficult holiday in the calendar is Christmas. It is the one holiday in the United States that *no one* can avoid. It is in the stores, streets, music, newspapers, magazines; it is on television, radio, in movie theaters and seemingly even in the air itself. The following are some suggestions to help people cope with holidays and anniversaries.

Tradition is made for people, not people for tradition. If the tradition no longer fits or is now uncomfortable, consider changing it. Perhaps it is time to begin a new tradition based on new circumstances.

If there is nothing to celebrate, do not force yourself. Let the day pass. It will come again next year and the next. The time will surely come when the desire to celebrate will return.

Grief saps the physical and emotional strength of the bereaved. This may be a time to make gentle excuses for missing that annual office party or family get-together. Don't push yourself. If you don't want to go, if you are too tired, stay home, rest and relax.

Restaurants stay open on most holidays knowing that some people will not want to prepare a large meal and clean up afterward. Consider eating out if you want to have a large meal. A quiet snack alone is also acceptable.

For many people in grief, returning to their place of worship can be painful, especially if that is where the funeral and/or memorial service was held. The ritual of the services, the music, prayers, and even members of the congregation can bring back the sorrow. For some, it is important they attend these services, despite the pain.

It is not uncommon for people to try to buy their way out of grief. This is particularly true when a parent dies, and other family members seem ready to buy every toy in the city for the children, as if toys could ever replace Mommy or Daddy. Adults do it for themselves, too, buying new furniture, clothes, or perhaps taking an extravagant weekend trip. This is a time to watch your spending.

HOSPICE OF BEND, OREGON[3]

Make a list of some traditions you want to hold on to that once included the person who died. It might be making that creamy chocolate fudge or pulling taffy, having oyster stew after church on Christmas Eve or singing carols.

1. _____

2. _____

3. _____

4. _____

After Joan died, Patrick dreaded the long-standing Thanksgiving celebration with his mother-in-law and all of Joan's family. *How will I survive?* he wondered.

However, his mother-in-law surprised him by renting several motel units at the Oregon Coast. Patrick was surrounded by the people who cared about him without being in the familiar surroundings, and it was very helpful.

Which traditions will you let go?

1. _____

2. _____

3. _____

4. _____

Jane's family insisted her Christmas be happy and upbeat. They didn't want to talk about her teenage son, Joshua, who had died a few months before. "It was like saying he never existed," Jane wrote and read to her journaling group.

Then a friend brought her a twenty-four-hour burning candle. Jane lit the candle on Joshua's grave and was comforted that it would burn through the hours she would struggle to not say his name. Without a word spoken, it flickered, "I remember."

Another grieving mother wrote "I Hate Christmas" in huge, scrawling, childlike letters over the page of her journal. It was honest. It was how she felt at that time. Like all of us, she found that the holidays always come around no matter what else happens in life.

What will help you get through the holidays?

_____

_____

_____

Which coming special day do you dread the most? Why?

_____

_____

_____

I remember feeling such loss on Valentine's Day because I was no longer anyone's sweetheart. My friend, Janine, said, "My dad never missed Valentine's Day by bringing me candy. Who will bring it now?"

A widowed man had a different concern. He wrote, "Mother's Day had always been a special, honored day in our home; a day we all took our special lady out to dinner. I thought that maybe, if I didn't remind my children of the day, they would forget it and I could bear the hurt by myself.

"After church, on the way to the car, one of them said, 'This is Mother's Day; aren't we going out to dinner?'

"They hadn't forgotten their mother, or the fact that their dad was trying so hard to fill her shoes." [4]

On this page describe how you would like to spend the coming holidays.

_____

_____

_____

_____

_____

_____

_____

What is keeping you from realizing this desire?

_____

_____

_____

_____

_____

DO THEY CELEBRATE CHRISTMAS IN HEAVEN?

As I sat by my window, day dreaming, one rainy December day,
It didn't seem possible that Christmas could be just a few days away.
I closed my eyes for a moment, or so it seemed to me;
Then I began seeing pictures in the light from my Christmas tree.
I saw myself up in heaven standing on streets of gold.
I saw the mansions all lighted with a soft and shimmering glow.
As I stood there in awe, and all breathless, I saw Gabriel coming my way,
"I've come to answer your question," he said. "That's why you are here today."
"Yes indeed, we celebrate Christmas; we remember the Holy Child's birth;
Our pageant is very much the same as yours is down on the earth.
The same wise men who journeyed coming from lands afar,
Join us each year in the pageant, but they don't need the light of the star.
The same shepherds who came to the manger will worship with us today,
They, too, come each year and gladly; nothing could keep them away.
We have no place for the innkeeper, but let me make one thing clear,
He had no room for the Christ Child, and that's why he is not here.

The same angel choir will gather and the bells of heaven
will ring.
Why even the littlest angel is always allowed to sing.
There will be joy and gladness, laughter, music, and
song.
I'll even blow my trumpet to summon the happy throng.
We'll not worship the babe in the manger, but the Christ
who sits on the throne;
We will praise, love, and adore Him. We're so glad to
have Him back home."
I listened with awe and wonder; my heart was filled with
delight.
I just had to ask him a question, "Why don't you have it
at night?"
As he looked at me his eyes twinkled, as he said, "You
forget my dear;
We can't have it then for a reason, remember? We have
no night up here."
I don't know how long I dreamed there, but when I
opened my eyes,
The rain had turned to sunshine, and a rainbow filled the
sky.
I know you'll never believe this, but I saw Gabriel
standing there,
Where the rainbow dipped from the skyways, at the foot
of the golden stairs.
I saw him smile as the rainbow was slowly fading away,
And he called to me, "Merry Christmas. Make it a Holy
Day."[5]

Thoughts about Special Days

Today as you read and write and listen to your heart, do you realize you have scaled a mountain? I hope you are pleased with yourself for sticking to your commitment to keep climbing (even if you occasionally skin your shins) until you find a place to unload and come to grips with your sorrow.

Many of you have made new friends because of the changes in who you are now. And some of you honored a commitment to take this journey with a friend and support each other over the finish line. Good for you!

Use the rest of this page to make notes about the ways of handling special days your friends and family have brought to your attention.

_____

_____

_____

_____

_____

_____

_____

A Christmas Gift for Me

I opened a Christmas card to find a photo of my husband and me. The note said, "This may possibly be the last picture taken of you and Dick together. I thought you might like to have it. Love, Cleo."

I studied the picture for a long time. His arm hung on my shoulder; my arm curled around his waist. Yes, I remembered. It was taken on the west bank of Klamath Lake two months before he died. Four of us had gone for a Sunday afternoon ride, a picnic, a time of sharing and laughter. And Cleo brought her camera.

I studied that picture over and over. It reminded me how much taller he was than me. I had almost forgotten that one dark front tooth until I looked closely at the photo again. Instantly, I knew I had begun to heal.

I pictured myself dropping my arm from his waist to begin my new journey, alone, to the other side of the lake. That would be the Christmas gift I would give myself.[6]

You will know you're beginning to recover when:

- Taking care of yourself is not only OK, but it feels good.
- The future is not so frightening.
- You can handle "special days" without falling apart.
- You want to reach out to others in need or in pain.
- Your emotional roller coaster is slowing down.
- You skip or forget a ritual such as visiting the cemetery without guilt.[7]

For six weeks or more you have been journaling about your loss and grief and pain. By now you must suspect that there is life after bereavement. There is light at the end of this grief tunnel. Your eyes can now begin to focus on goals, soloing, and hopefully, recovery. Are you ready?

The Aroma of Recovery

I'm not sure if it's the eating or the aroma that inspired me to bake zucchini bread so often. It certainly was tasty, but the blending of spices, nuts, and dates seemed to linger in the air a little longer than most of the baking I did.

Coming in the door, my husband would hesitate, sniff upward and smile. I could always count on the same comment at the dinner table. "I just don't understand why you call that bread," he would say. "That's not bread; that's cake."

After he died, I realized that baking goodies was one of the many things I did for him that I truly enjoyed doing. Now there is no one to make that ritualistic comment; no one to stand at the back door and breathe in the scrumptious scents from the oven, no one to tease me about "fattening him up."

Then one day it happened. For some reason I was so hungry I was ravenous. I was consumed with a desire for zucchini bread, moist and nutty and sweet scented. Finally yielding to my craving, I reached for the bowl and mixer. I not only baked two loaves, but I ate several slices while it was still hot. Then I purposely went outside and returned, inhaling deeply, savoring the fragrance that filled every nook and cranny. "That's not bread; that's cake!" I laughed aloud. Here again, I recognized that healing was taking place.[8]

Some things I'm thinking, feeling, wishing, hoping, doing:

Date: _____

_____

_____

_____

_____

_____

_____

_____

_____

_____

_____

_____

_____

Moving On

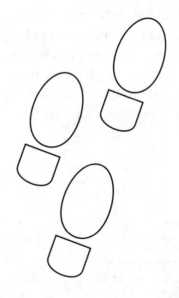

The Power of a Dream

"I have a dream" said Martin Luther King Jr.[1] Everyone needs to have a dream. Dreams, like goals, are necessary to carry you forward from day to day; they keep you on the proper road to get where you're going. Without dreams and goals, we'd grow lazy and sullen, and, soon, life would hold no purpose.

Inhale deeply. In every breath of life there lies a purpose for you alone—exciting and exhilarating enough to give you momentum to pursue dreams with a passion and to reinvest in goals that have lain dormant.

This session is for dreamers—people who set goals, wish on stars, and look for rainbows. In choosing to move on, you have chosen to step out of the dark to turn the corner and shout for all the world to hear, "I am a survivor!"

Think about and note a time you realized you were beginning to heal.

_____

_____

_____

_____

_____

_____

_____

Make two lists—one of short-term goals you'd like to reach in the next one to three months, and the other of long-term goals set for the next one to three years.

Example: Short-term goals

- Learn to wash my own wool shirts.
- Go out to lunch by myself.
- Be faithful with my daily devotions.
- Have a guest over for dinner.
- Attend a grief recovery class.
- Forgive the one responsible for the tragedy in my life.

Example: Long-term goals

- Trade my car in for a new one.
- Have another baby.
- Lose excess weight or quit smoking.
- Take classes at the local community college.
- Join a drama group or church choir.
- Visit someone else's mom at a nursing home.

Short-term goals:

_____

_____

_____

_____

_____

Long-term goals:

_____

_____

_____

_____

_____

_____

Describe how or when you can begin to work on some of your goals.

_____

_____

_____

_____

_____

_____

They told me one day I would go twenty-four hours without thinking of my loss. I told them they were crazy.

They weren't crazy; they were right. At first, I felt guilt, then elation. I was getting ready to solo.

Soloing is done without the companionship of another. For many widowed, living alone is the first step to gaining a proper perspective to who they are. For those who married right out of high school or college, being thrust into widowhood is their first time to solo.

For those whose parents have died, you are orphans. Finally, you are "the old folks" of the family. Hold your head high and solo!

The long walk into your first PTA meeting or children's Sunday school class since your child died is one of the longest walks you'll ever take. No one can take that solo journey for you. There are no prizes for spectators, only participants.

I will seek the Lord to renew my strength.
I will soar on wings like eagles.
I will run but not be weary; walk and not grow faint.
I will solo and not be lonely.
ISAIAH 40:31 (AUTHOR'S PARAPHRASE)

There is value in soloing. In an airplane, you must first know the controls and who controls them. In life after bereavement, the same principle applies.

No matter what you do for the first time, it's important that you reach out to take the hand of the One who said He would never leave you. He'll walk beside you, and His strength and stamina will flow through your veins. And when you tire, He'll carry you. Let Him.

A Step of Faith

By now, you must suspect that healing and peace are not found in your circumstances but in the way you relate to your circumstances. Whatever you place as the god of your life will dictate your sense of peace and well-being.

Peace is often sought but many times not found by the bereaved because they look for someone to give it to them. However, it comes only from within, from a relationship with Jesus Christ. If you haven't taken that step of faith to ask Jesus to forgive you for your past, to fill the void in your life today, and take you to His heaven when you die, I invite you to do that right now. That act will be the most important step you take toward moving on, surviving, celebrating, and reinvesting in the rest of your life.

It is as simple as this prayer: Jesus, the Bible says You died on a cross to pay the penalty for my sins and then lived again after three days. I believe that. I believe that You are the Son of God and I want You to come into my life, forgive my sins, and give me the desire to live a life pleasing to You. From now on, I will look to You for love, forgiveness, and guidance. Thank You for Your gift of eternal life and for Your Holy Spirit who has now come to live in me to show me how to walk with You for the rest of my life. Amen.

If you prayed that prayer, write the date here _____.
I hope you'll tell someone who will rejoice with you. Who will you share the good news with?_____

_____

_____

The best time of your life may be yet to follow because you took this step of faith. Don't depend on feelings or emotions. Your life will not be without loss or pain or problems, but now you'll have a new source of strength to get you through them.

"For I know the plans I have for you,"
declares the LORD, "plans to prosper you and not to
harm you, plans to give you hope and a future.
Then you will call upon me and come and
pray to me, and I will listen to you.
You will seek me and find me
when you seek me with all your heart."

JEREMIAH 29:11–13

There is life beyond bereavement. That's a discovery worth celebrating, don't you think? How will you celebrate this week?

List some ways you can celebrate:

- Invite a friend to a ballgame.
- Buy some new sheets.
- Share a banana-split with a friend.
- Sit in a hot tub.
- Cook dinner in a wok.

_____

_____

_____

"*Tomorrow has two handles: the handle of fear and the handle of faith. You can take hold of it by either handle.*"[2]

Read the following quotation aloud:

> *I will greet this day with love in my heart.*
> *And how will I do this? Henceforth will I look on all things with love . . . I will love the sun for it warms my bones; yet I will love the rain for it cleanses my spirit.*
> *I will love the light for it shows me the way; yet I will love the darkness for it shows me the stars.*
> *I will welcome happiness for it enlarges my heart; yet I will endure sadness for it opens my soul.*
> *I will acknowledge rewards for they are my due; yet I will welcome obstacles for they are my challenge.*[3]

Describe your feelings as you read:

_____

_____

_____

_____

There are gifts to be found in each and every day. Shared in a glance . . . carried in a smile.

Gifts that become priceless when life is measured by the compassionate hand of God. He makes it possible to rediscover the joy of living one day at a time.

As you complete this journal, you have shown that grief can be met not only with dignity and purpose, but with richness of spirit that makes every moment count.

It has been a privilege to offer this unique resource and support for the bereaved believing it is possible to move on after the death of a loved one. It means taking the grief that is on the inside and sharing it on the outside.

To an Awesome God, I offer praise and honor and gratitude for leading the way.

Hugs!

BARBARA BAUMGARDNER

A hug is better than a new bathrobe or furry slippers. Hugs span the space between the heart and the soul to remind us we are alive.

DARCIE SIMS[4]

Epilogue

The last page of this book does not end your journey. Chances are good that you will find times when expressing your deepest feelings can best be done on paper.

I want to challenge you to continue journaling in another book, on another day, in a way that brings emotional release that is both restful and satisfying.

The years, months, and hours that remain in your life are yours to spend any way you choose. Do not waste them, but pursue the rest of your life without self-pity or discontent. When you discover purpose in living, your hopes and dreams will be filled with joy, peace, and love.

Above all else, I encourage you to walk with God. He is the ultimate source of healing for whatever is wrong in your life. That's because He loves you.

Poet Carl Sandburg said, "Life is like an onion; you peel it off one layer at a time, and sometimes you weep."

Weeping is often necessary to get to the core of our life.

Periods of our life make us weep—like that awful day when someone told you (and me) that someone dear to us was dead. Under the layers of tears, anguish, heartache, and doubts, it's hard to imagine finding a core that is sweet and desirable.

My prayer for you is that during the next few weeks, you will allow Jesus Christ to tap into each layer of your life to expose the grief and pain that brought you to this book. I pray that you will allow Him to touch you with the healing that can fill the void left by that someone special who died.

If weeping becomes necessary to get to that core, don't be embarrassed. Hopefully, you are with people who understand your sorrow. Be assured that God does, and so do I.

Barbara Baumgardner

CONGRATULATIONS!

This certifies that:

_____

has successfully completed A *Passage through Grief* program.

Group Leader: _____

Date: _____

May the God of hope fill you with all joy and peace as you trust in him, so that you may overflow with hope by the power of the Holy Spirit.

ROMANS 15:13

Leader's Guide

Introduction

Leading a grief journaling group can be an enjoyable and rewarding experience. It will also stretch and intimidate you, especially if you've never done it before.

Some experience in journaling and familiarity with the grief process will help you be an effective group leader. Other qualifications include a compassionate heart, a love for reading and writing, and a sincere desire to help hurting people.

Stability in your own emotions is also important to cope with the tears, anger, and loneliness that surface in a group of grieving people. Some bereavement training with an organization such as Hospice is very helpful. Without most of these characteristics, you may find the role of a grief-recovery facilitator is simply not your niche.

It is vital to remember that the men and women who attend any grief recovery group are extremely vulnerable. Caution should be exercised when offering advice, especially based on your own experiences. The people attending your group are looking to you for hope, not pat answers.

There is a significant increase in the rate of suicide among those who are mourning a loss. Watch for signs of unresolved conflict and ongoing depression. Don't hesitate to seek out professional help when the need arises, especially when the bereaved person continually writes or talks about having no reason or desire to live.

Got butterflies? Great! You are about to journey down an intriguing pathway into a world laced with pain and frustration; yet in spite of all the rocky obstacles, you will see miracles happen. As you touch the lives of others with this program of support and education, you will be touched also by their lives, their love, their kindness, and their respect and friendship.

Remember, it is usually the facilitator who learns the most—so step out, lead on, and grow!

My prayer for you as the leader:

Lord, I thank You for Your promise that You never leave us nor forsake us. I thank You that You want to take the sorrow and emotional pain from the lives of these who long for healing from the tragic loss of a loved one. I ask for that healing for each person who has had the courage to step out in this difficult time to say, "I need help. I need to learn to live with my loss."

I ask, Lord, that You will take charge of this class, that You will reshape lives and convert struggles into energy, prayer, and courage. Change these lives to see they can have value again. Show them how to look to You to fill their days and nights with peace and joy and healing.

And Lord, I ask You to equip this dear person to be a servant facilitator who will listen to Your leading and allow You to be the teacher and healer during these sessions.

We welcome Your presence in this grief recovery workshop.

In Your precious name, Amen.

Preparing for a Grief Journaling Group

Set a Date and Time

Early evening (6:30 to 8:00 P.M.) usually works well. Most older people will appreciate getting home early and people who work usually find this a good time. However, each group will vary, and you'll need to find the time that is comfortable for the majority. An hour and a half gives time for work but not much socializing.

Check local community calendars to be sure there is no holiday or other conflict with your choice of day. Try not to change the meeting time once it is established, as grieving people are often easily confused and forgetful. Begin and end the meeting on time.

Advertise

Put notices on community bulletin boards, in newsletters, and call mortuaries to tell them of your intent to lead a grief journaling group. Ask the special events reporter for your local newspaper to write a story. List your meeting in community events bulletins and in television and radio public service announcements.

Some churches will want help with the bereaved in their congregation, especially when the staff has no personal grief experience or even available lay people to come alongside those who are grieving. An announcement in church bulletins or newsletters may bring some bereaved to your journaling group.

(Warning: Don't get too many people in your group. Six is perfect; eight is workable, but more than that doesn't allow enough time for reading and sharing in an hour and a half to two hours.)

Be Prepared

Review the session notes and leader's guide before arriving at meeting location. A lonely journaler may arrive early, distracting you from what you planned to be your study time. Advance preparation also gives you time to thoughtfully consider what might be the reaction of the journalers to the material you will be presenting. How can you encourage them to take the risk of sharing their innermost feelings with those around them?

Plan for your time to be disrupted by emotion and by those who need to talk. On the other hand, if the group is non-communicative, you may find you have extra time.

Consider ways to fill that time with hope. Suggestions are given with each session.

Participants will need to have their own copy of the book, *A Passage through Grief*, to read and write in. It works well for group leaders to purchase the required number of copies prior to the first meeting and then ask to be reimbursed for the cost. However, a leader may request that the participants purchase their own copy at a bookstore prior to the first meeting. Give your local Christian bookstore at least two weeks' notice so they can have enough copies on hand for your group.

A break is usually not appropriate in the middle of these sessions as it stops the flow of communicating feelings. As participants begin to bond and share, extra time may be needed for socializing after the session ends.

Welcome, Warmth and Encouragement Are Vital

Remember, journaling is not for everyone and most people will feel intimidated. A soft drink, coffee, or tea with a cookie can ease the tension and calm the fears before the first session. Simple refreshments should be ready so that valuable class time is not used for preparation or waiting for coffee or water to heat. People can finish eating during the session.

If someone had a bad week, mail a note of encouragement or telephone the person between sessions.

Always be on the lookout for outside sources of help: articles, stories, bookmarks, poems, or greeting cards to share with the group as "extra treats."

During the Session

One of the major jobs of a facilitator is to pace the study. Open with a sincere interest in what kind of week group members have had. One woman excitedly reported that for the first time since her husband's death seven months ago, she had all her bills paid. The group rejoiced with her.

Ask questions that draw them into discussion. This will enable them to be comfortable with reading aloud. A journaler found the courage to write about her angry, rebellious son after being asked how this son was dealing with the loss of his father. She was relieved to find it was OK to share her pain.

Each session has a suggested opening in the journaling workbook. Read this aloud. Ask questions such as "How did that make you feel?" or "Tell me how you identify with that," or "Has this happened to you?"

Review the list of "ground rules" on pages 114–115 as often as appropriate. A quick review of rules can be a gentle reminder that one person should not dominate the time and deprive others of an opportunity to share.

Those attending these journaling sessions may want to hear bits and pieces of your story to know you as a person, not just as the facilitator. Your human side, your downfalls as well

110

as victories with your own journey through grief, can be shared briefly. This will help them to know that you truly can relate to their loss.

The group facilitator does not read from his or her own journal. Keep in mind that your job is to help group members discover ways to keep from "stuffing" their grief. Journaling is one of their tools. They need to focus on their own healing, not on you.

Let the workbook help you moderate discussions, draw in the more quiet members, and pace the study. Encourage people to interact and share their observations. Volunteer your own reactions *only* to offer encouragement and hope.

Make notes while participants read from their journals. Use them as guidelines for discussion such as, "You wrote about never telling your mother she was beautiful. Is there some way you can do that now?" Or, "Were you angry at him for dying or for leaving you alone?" Encourage group participation.

Be alert to particular needs in the group. Sometimes you may need to abandon even the best laid plans to deal with "emotion emergencies." When other group members comfort and support a distraught member, a few minutes of the session may be lost, but important bonding and friendships are gained.

Contact with one another outside the meeting can be as valuable as the meeting itself.

After three or four sessions, a luncheon could be scheduled for the entire group. As a leader, you do not need to feel compelled to attend. It is important for the bereaved to find support away from you.

Review the list of additional resources and suggested reading at the end of the book when you find you have time to fill.

Suggest that the bereaved check out the local library or area hospice for books or videos on grief.

Christian bookstores often will have a good selection of books on grief, and most are willing to order specific books.

A word of caution if you recommend books to your group: Know the contents of the book. For example, *Helping People through Grief* by Delores Kuenning is for the caregiver who wants to help people in pain and crisis. It is not intended for the grieving person. *A Widow's Guide to Living Alone* by Judith Fabisch would not be as appropriate for a widower as *A Tearful Celebration* by James E. Means.

The following pages will lead you through all of the sessions in this book. You will see how some of your own grief experiences are helpful as you follow the leader's guide through each class as outlined. You will learn to leave out what is not appropriate for your unique group.

Bon voyage! Have a wonderful and satisfying journey as you lead the bereaved beside still waters to a peaceful place called Hope.

Session 1

Introduce yourself as the facilitator. Pass around a sign-in sheet and name tags.

Encourage large, printed names that can be seen across the table. Read or explain the following in your own words:

For session 1, I will do much of the talking except to have you introduce yourselves so we can begin to know each other. But next time, it's your turn and I won't talk so much.

It has taken a lot of courage for you to come. It is hard to come to a group when you might not know anyone, but even harder when you are dealing with a personal loss. Today is the hardest time. When you get ready to come next week, the anxiety you are feeling now won't be as severe because you'll know more of what to expect when you walk into the room.

Please don't let your apprehension get in your way of participating and benefiting from this group. (Note: If you want to lead the group in some deep breathing or relaxing exercises, now would be the time to do that. You might find it helpful to have an ice-breaker activity.)

It is important that you attend regularly. I'm asking you to make a commitment to be here, not only for yourself but for the other group members. However, if you must miss, do that session at home so you can keep up with the rest of the group.

Review these weekly sessions at home. Read them over and over if necessary. You may not understand all the information given, so I encourage you to ask questions during the meetings.

When we finish six or seven weeks from now, we will have examined a lot of grief recovery helps, along with the grief journaling. Hopefully, you will have recognized some signs of recovery.

Beginning today, you are going to make some new friends—some you may have for the rest of your life. This will not be a confrontational group—our approach is one of gentleness and acceptance. We encourage participation because you will benefit more if you are involved. But we recognize that quiet people get a lot out of these groups as well as the more talkative ones.

Reactions to the writing you do will be nonjudgmental. You see, grief is unique to each individual. We all *own* our own feelings; it is not our job to give advice or criticize one another.

However, if you have any stories, poems, or letters that have helped you in the grief process, please feel free to bring them and as time permits, you may share them. I don't have all the answers so your sharing may benefit us all.

We do have some "Ground Rules." (Note: Read aloud unless you make a copy for each person. If so, have each person read one aloud.)

1. *Confidentiality is essential.* We may hear and share some personal and private information. To feel safe, we need to know what we share doesn't go outside this group. We will be trusting others with a piece of our hearts.

2. *It is OK to say "pass."* You are not obligated to talk or share if you feel uncomfortable doing so.

3. *We speak for and about ourselves only.* We are here to deal with our own grief, not that of another person.

4. *Everyone should have an opportunity to share.* One of the roles of the facilitator is to make sure no one talks too long. The facilitator may become a "timekeeper."

If anyone needs to talk about something privately and you are not comfortable bringing it up in the group session, you may call me for an appointment. If I can't help, I may suggest you see a counselor or a pastor.

5. *We will allow newcomers next week only.* After the second week, the group is closed. If you must drop out, a telephone call would be considerate to let your fellow members know.

6. *Know that feelings and emotions will surface during our time together.* It is OK to cry. Healing occurs through expressing and sharing our feelings. (Note: A box or two of tissues should be within reach.)

Turn to page 3 and follow along while I read it aloud. It explains the process of journaling your grief. (It also works well to ask each person to read a paragraph aloud here. Watch for boredom as you read to them. Minds are on overload here and they need to participate as much as possible.)

Introduce yourself briefly again and tell only about your loss. Ask others to share what brought them here (if they can) and what they hope to get out of this group.

Turn to page 5 as you begin and as needed throughout introductions. Use it as a reference for those who have difficulty telling about their loss.

Allow about thirty minutes for a group of six people to share. (Take notes for future reference about their losses or needs.) Call attention to the quote on page 6.

If you have less than fifteen minutes before ending this session, just walk through the rest of the pages in session 1 with the group. Explain how pages 6–8 will help get them started writing something to be read aloud next week. It need not be long, but encourage them to write something.

Make sure the group knows that the writing examples in the workbook are from previous journaling groups and are included as encouragement for those who follow.

When you get to "The Dance" by Thelda Bevens, explain to the group that she is an English teacher and that you do not expect them to write so professionally. Remind them that a short piece like the one written by Maryal Beauvais is equally effective.

If you have men in your group, affirm their willingness to face their grief head-on. Read aloud "Men and Grief" and the notes done by Elie if time permits.

Use the following two pages to close session 1, or to fill extra time in another session:

Why Grief Recovery Is Important

Someone's death brings a lot of pain and loss and change.

This can produce bitterness and illness, but *support* plus *pain* plus *change* produces growth.

Many people "stuff" their pain by trying to keep very busy. Others run away from the pain while some may get married to try to avoid it. But the sooner and more intensely you mourn the loss, the sooner you will heal.

Results of unresolved grief:

- When a child dies, 50 to 80 percent of the parents will be divorced within one year.

- People who experience a major grief loss have a 600 percent increase in illness or hospitalization.

- With a sudden death, there is a significantly higher percentage of a second death of someone who is grief stricken within eighteen months.

- The immune system doesn't function very well when people go through intense grief.

- There is an increase in vandalism, delinquency, alcohol consumption, illicit relationships, and suicide among both the young and old.

116

✿ An earlier unresolved loss makes it more difficult to resolve current losses (even the loss of a family pet).

With a support system, these trends are reversed.

Wendy Howard, LCW, former Social Services director at the Hospice of Bend, always used this analogy in her grief recovery sessions: "After a major car accident, bones take time to heal. The body might need special diet, equipment, therapy, and time before going back to work. Grief is similar to that."

When grief is stuffed, or buried, it waits for us. It will come up at a later time, and that may be an even more difficult time to deal with it.

What Things Make It Difficult for People to Grieve?

✿ Mobility and up-rootedness of American society (families scattered).

✿ Lack of support systems.

✿ People saying, "Hurry up and get well." They feel we should be "over it" in two or three weeks.

✿ We teach our kids not to express their losses so how then, as an adult, can we be expected to express our loss in an emotionally bankrupt society?

✿ We've been sheltered from death—we don't see death around us and tend to deny it. We have had no examples to learn from.

✿ Increased secularization. We have been removed from our faith and our rituals or symbols of grief (no sackcloth and ashes or periods of mourning).

117

- More and more, we see newspaper obituaries that read, "No services will be held at the request of the deceased," thereby denying people of an opportunity to say "good-bye."

- The deaths we don't talk about are suicide and abortion.

- We don't know what to expect, what is normal or acceptable emotions and behavior.

Invite participants to share feelings and reactions concerning grief they have experienced.

Session 2

Introduce any new participants. Briefly introduce returning journalers by name and loss, and then quickly review the last session. (New members should do session 1 at home rather than the entire group having to do the session over.)

Before reading journals aloud, encourage participants to begin to talk by sharing about their past week. A simple, "How was your week?" or "Did you have any problems writing?" should prepare them to read aloud for the first time.

Ask for a volunteer to read from her journal. If no one offers, pick a person you believe will do it with ease. Take notes and encourage discussion between each reading.

Turn to session 2: Discuss changes that come after a significant person dies. See pages 24–25. Then take turns reading aloud from pages 26–27, "Ten Stages of Grief."

Assign "stages" as a topic for journaling this week. Remember to inform the group that topic assignments are only suggestions. If participants feel the need to write about something else, they are free to do so. Suggest that they write more than one time during the week, especially when they are feeling emotional or depressed.

The rest of this session may be used to discuss the stages of grief or the page of "Gifts to Give Yourself." Encourage participants to re-read the pages at home. If suicide is a factor for anyone in your group, you may want to read aloud page 32. If you have participants who think their catastrophic grief experience is worse than others, try to level the playing field. If reading Scripture doesn't help, you may have some ideas of your own. Ask for permission to share a list of names and telephone numbers at the next session.

Session 3

Distribute the list of names and telephone numbers of consenting participants.

It is common for people to find encouragement in one another's writing. Group members may ask each other for copies. That's OK. Sharing losses and celebrating victories pave the way to survival. If no copy equipment is available on site, ask the writer to make copies and bring them next time if she is comfortable doing that. The recipients may want to offer to reimburse her the five or ten cents each copy costs.

Be sure to tell participants that it's OK to say no if they don't want to share copies of their work. A woman whose son died from AIDS wrote a very touching letter to her son as an assignment for session 3. Many asked for a copy, but it was such a delicate piece of her heart she couldn't give it away.

Take turns reading the journaling done during the past week. Follow the same instructions for discussions as suggested in session 2. When finished, discuss letter writing and begin session 3.

The facilitator or group members should read some of the letters given as examples in session 3. Discuss the ideas for letter writing listed on page 38.

The facilitator should read the letter by Ellen Rollins on pages 41 and 42, as it always evokes emotions. Sometimes, one person's journaling will seem to reveal a deeper intensity of grief than that expressed by others. This can have a minimizing effect on the grief of some in the group.

Remind them that there is no stereotypical person in grief. There is no right or wrong feeling or behavior, or more painful grief for one than another. *All feelings are* OK. Some people just express them more openly and intensely.

Page 42, "His Part, Our Part," offers an opportunity to discuss an aspect of grief that Christians often avoid. Allow for time to talk about how bondage can block healing.

Suggest participants make a list of supports or supporters to review when they feel all alone. Include helpful family members, friends, neighbors, counselors, and even pets. Such a list can show that they are not as alone as they may feel. However, be aware of anyone who may need extra attention (new in town, no relatives, etc.).

Remind the group of the blank page at the end of each session called, "Some things I'm thinking, feeling, wishing, hoping, doing." Encourage them to use these pages to write down any feelings they have, even those feelings of anger and disbelief.

If time allows, read and discuss the "Goals of Grief Recovery." Before dismissing remind the participants their homework for the coming week is to write a letter.

Session 4

"How was your week?" is always a good way to open the session. It shouldn't take a lot of time, but it shows that you care about what is going on in their lives.

The questions on pages 50–51 will lead into reading aloud.

Encourage group members to take notes about each other. You should allow enough time to read over the poetry in the workbook and examine the photo and sketch pages. Call attention to the importance of completing the assignment on pages 56–57 for the next session. Participants usually are not only willing but anxious to share their photos. It is a time to put faces on those people they've been talking and writing about.

Affirm any bonding and support that has taken place between individuals in the group.

Now is a good time to remind the group that this is the halfway point of the sessions. Encourage friendships and telephone calls within the group, as well as to friends and family members. This will help participants learn to depend on other support systems away from this group.

Session 5

This may be one of your most special sessions. You and the others will be privileged to see photos and drawings. You may hear some poetry wrenched from pain deep within the soul. There may be laughter and tears as memories and creativity are shared.

Don't rush through this because healing is taking place.

Ask questions as the photos are passed. Encourage participants to tell something cute, funny, or memorable about their loved one.

Encourage others to ask questions before moving on to the next person. This allows everyone some time in the spotlight. Remember, sharing can be time consuming. When everyone is finished, begin session 5.

Many journalists have probably already talked or written about the words that seem difficult to say: *death, widow, lonely.* They've probably discussed many "firsts." As you are the one who knows the conversations that have already taken place, you'll need to decide if you want to ask them to read pages 62 to 63 on being "labeled" in class or at home, or if an around-the-table discussion would be more appropriate at this time.

If time allows, work together on pages 64 to 65.

Read aloud from page 66 and do the exercise on page 67, "Note Some of Your Firsts." An around-the-table discussion is usually both helpful and humorous here.

Assign page 70 as the homework for the week.

Have you been hugging and encouraging hugs at the end of each session?

Marcia Plows, on staff at Hospice of Bend, Oregon, says we need seven hugs a day to survive. Are you doing your part?

After his wife died, John Johnson jokingly commented, "The only time I get touched anymore is when I go to the chiropractor or the masseuse." While that might invoke a chuckle, there may be people in your group who feel exactly the same way.

Session 6

You will need to introduce "closure" in this session. No doubt you have established a trusting relationship with the participants in this group which makes it difficult to say good-bye. Do this very carefully. Death already has brought feelings of abandonment to these survivors, so care must be exercised to avoid the impression that you are abandoning them.

Encourage them to continue writing in their journals after the sessions are over. Remind them that they may need to make the first move—reaching out to those friends who didn't know what to say. Begin by making a telephone call, inviting a friend to lunch, organizing a hike or an evening at the movies. Suggest that those without family support spend birthdays and holidays with a friend.

Ask if they are in touch with their church or synagogue. Is it time to rejoin a bowling team, a bridge club, or take a class at the local college? Some may need a list of community activities or senior services.

Have a list of resources available for those who may need additional grief support.

Validation is a major need for anyone dealing with a death loss. Grieving people need reassurance that they are still special, valuable, and worthy—that life goes on even if they are no longer the mate, parent, or child of the one who died.

In this session and the next, be sure to thank the participants for the way they have touched and enriched your life. Tell them you are proud of them and the progress they've made. By the end of this journey, most will have discovered that even though they can't turn back the clock, they can now wind it up again on their own.

Ask how many accomplished a "first" thing this week.

Some lists of "first" things might be long and include some specific needs.

Remind participants to take notes of ways they can help each other in such tasks as finding where to get the oil changed, or how to cook a turkey.

Turn in your book to session 6. Most grieving people dread facing the holidays without the one who died more than any other thing they must face. However, many have admitted afterwards that the "dreading it" was *worse* than the "doing it." Pages 79–80 are good pages to read aloud. Stress that it is OK to not hang on to the same old traditions and to let the day pass if needed. If time allows, work through pages 80–83 in class.

Remind journalers that special days do not include only Thanksgiving and Christmas, birthdays and anniversaries. There will be the anniversary of the day your loved one died, Valentine's Day, Labor Day, and if the loss was a child, there will be the Prom, Graduation, and many special children's holidays. Discuss these as time allows.

Pass out some copies of articles on dealing with grief during the holidays that you have on hand. Watch magazines for helpful articles to make copies of, but remember to write to the publisher or author for permission to do this. Most are copyrighted, making it unlawful to use the material without prior permission.

In the beginning, we sometimes refer to session 7 as an "optional session."

By this time most have probably decided if they want to continue with this group for the seventh session or whether to finish with this one. Encourage them to finish.

Even if the bereaved aren't ready to put the past behind, it is nice to know how.

"Moving On," "Setting Goals," and "Soloing" will offer guidelines to consider in days ahead.

Remember: There may be some who still have so much grief to deal with that they are unable to even think about moving on. If so, encourage them to do session 7 at home at a later time. Others will want you to walk with them through this last session of their journaling journey.

For those who will not return for session 7, make a Certificate of Completion similar to the one at the end of session 7 and give it to them before saying "good-bye." Don't forget the hug.

Session 7

Congratulate the returning participants for being willing to "move on." It takes courage to face an uncertain future head-on.

Try to take less than thirty minutes to hear what was written about holidays and special days.

Turn to session 7 and ask the group to follow as you read page 92. Spend some time talking about times when participants felt that healing was beginning for them.

Work on the lists of short-term and long-term goals on page 94 during this session. Allow about ten minutes of quiet time for members to write down some of their goals. Encourage them to discuss what they have written with the group. Ask questions like, "How and when will you begin working on this goal?" "What help do you need or can you do this alone?"

Talk about soloing and celebrating accomplished goals. Encourage them to tell someone about their victory. Ask each person to commit to doing something fun for themselves within the next seven days.

This entire session should be done in class. Make it an upbeat meeting. Serve special refreshments or decorate the room before participants arrive.

Shake hands with each person as you give them a Certificate of Completion.

Follow that with a hug!

Again, encourage participants to stay in touch. Suggest they go back and read what they wrote in the early sessions to see how far they have come. Close this session by praying for each person individually if you are comfortable doing that.

You will need to emotionally and physically detach from your group at this point if you plan to continue facilitating grief recovery groups. Explain to the participants, if necessary, that you want them to find support and fellowship in each other, releasing you to re-invest your heart, time, and emotions in another group of hurting people.

Your help, love, and caring attitude will spread through the community long after this journaling session is finished. If you want to stay in touch or give permission for anyone to contact you, make that decision before saying "good-bye."

Your gift to the bereaved has no doubt helped them to begin healing. However, God is the only one who can completely fill the void left by the person who died.

Encourage participants to find a Bible study or get involved in their churches.

Congratulations and thank you for helping others rediscover the joy of living after the death of someone they loved.

If you have questions or comments, you may write the author.

Barbara Baumgardner
2632 N. E. Rosemary Drive
Bend, OR 97701-9514
E-mail: barbarab@bendcable.com

Leader's Notes

_____

_____

_____

_____

_____

_____

_____

_____

_____

_____

_____

_____

_____

Suggested Reading

AARP (American Association of Retired Persons). *On Being Alone: A Guide for Widowed Persons*. Washington, D.C., 1988.

Graham, Billy. *Death and the Life After*. Dallas, Texas: Word Publishing, 1987.

Heavilin, Marilyn Willett. *Roses in December* and *December's Song: Finding Strength within Grief*. San Bernardino, Calif.: Here's Life Publishers, 1986, 1988.

Hewitt, John H. *After Suicide*. Philadelphia, Pa.: The Westminster Press, 1980.

Kübler-Ross, Elisabeth. *On Death and Dying*. New York, N.Y.: MacMillan Publishing Co., Inc., 1969. And *Death: The Final Stages of Growth*. New York, N.Y.: Simon & Schuster, Inc., 1975.

Lewis, C. S. *A Grief Observed*. New York, N.Y.: The Seabury Press, 1963.

Osgood, Judy. *Meditations for the Widowed*. Sunriver, Oreg.: Gilgal Publications, 1985.

Kreis, Bernadine and Alice Pattie. *Up from Grief: Patterns of Recovery*. Minneapolis, Minn.: Seabury Press, 1969.

Mitsch, Raymond R. and Lynn Brookside. *Grieving the Loss of Someone You Love*. Ann Arbor, Mich.: Servant Publications, 1993.

Staudacher, Carol. *Men and Grief: A Guide for Men*. Oakland, Calif.: New Harbinger Publications, Inc., 1991.

Westberg, Granger. *Good Grief*. Minneapolis, Minn.: Fortress Press, 1962.

For Bereaved Parents

Kolf, June Cerza. *Grandma's Tears*. Grand Rapids, Mich.: Baker Books, 1995.

Osgood, Judy. *Meditations for Bereaved Parents*. Sunriver, Oreg.: Gilgal Publications, 1983.

Schiff, H. S. *The Bereaved Parent*. New York, N.Y.: Crown Publishers, Inc., 1977.

White, Mary A. *Harsh Grief, Gentle Hope*. Colorado Springs, Colo.: NavPress, 1995.

Helping Children

Coleman, William L. *When Someone You Love Dies*. Minneapolis, Minn.: Augsburg Press, 1994.

Dodd, Robert V. *Helping Children Cope with Death*. Kitchener, Ontario: Herald Press, 1984.

Libby, Larry. *Someday Heaven*. Sisters, Oreg.: Questar Publishers, Inc., 1993.

Sanford, Doris. *It Must Hurt a Lot: A Child's Book about Death*. Portland, Oreg.: Multnomah Press, 1986.

For Helping Others

Kuenning, Delores. *Helping People through Grief*. Minneapolis, Minn.: Bethany House Publishers, 1987.

Manning, Doug. *Comforting Those Who Grieve*. New York, N.Y.: Harper & Row, 1985.

Notes

Session 1

1. Reverend Paul Irion, D.D., "A Death Has Occurred," used by permission. Irion is Professor Emeritus of Pastoral Theology, Advisory Board for *Journeys* newsletter.

2. Judy Osgood, "Putting Grief into Words," adapted from article in *Compassionate Friends* newsletter, used by permission of author.

3. Wayne E. Oates, *Your Particular Grief* (Philadelphia, Pa.: The Westminster Press, 1981).

4. Kahlil Gibran, *The Wisdom of Gibran* (Philosophical Library) quoted in "Quotable Quotes," *Reader's Digest* (March 1983).

5. Thelda Bevens, "The Dance," used by permission.

6. Peter Marshall, *Mr. Jones, Meet the Master: Sermons and Prayers* (Grand Rapids: Fleming H. Revell Co., 1949), 16.

7. Maryal Beauvais, "Auntie Mildred's Nightgown," used by permission.

8. Sherwood Wirt and Kersten Beckstrom, *Quotation from Topical Encyclopedia of Living Quotations* (Bethany House Publishers), 126:1705.

9. Elie Bourque, "Elie's Journal," used by permission.

10. Thelda Bevens, "Bits and Pieces," used by permission.

11. Sybil Gibson, "Bits and Pieces," used by permission.

12. Suzanne McElroy, "Bits and Pieces," used by permission.

13. Maryal Beauvais, "Bits and Pieces," used by permission.

Session 2

1. C. S. Lewis, source unknown.

2. Adapted and reprinted from Granger Westburg, *Good Grief* (Fortress Press, 1962), used by permission of Augsburg Fortress.

3. Heinrich Heine, quoted in *Instant Quotation Dictionary* (Mundelein, Ill.: Career Institute), 9.

4. John Greenleaf Whittier, quoted in *Instant Quotation Dictionary* (Mundelein, Ill.: Career Institute), 223.

5. Barbara Baumgardner, "A Season of Suicide," *Meditations for the Widowed*, Judy Osgood, editor (Sunriver, Oreg.: Gilgal Publications), hereafter referred to by author's name and followed by *Meditations*.

Session 3

1. Pat Wester, "My Dearest Love," used by permission.

2. John Bunyan, quoted in *Meditations*, 41.

3. Barbara Baumgardner, "Dear Dick."

4. Chinese proverb, source unknown.

5. Ellen Rollins, "A Letter to My Daughter," used by permission.

Session 4

1. Cynthia G. Kelley, "Grief Is Like a River," *Compassionate Friends* newsletter, Cincinnati, Ohio, chapter of Compassionate Friends, used by permission.

2. Sybil S. Gibson, "Loss of My Beloved Husband," used by permission.

3. Terry Kittering, "There's an Elephant in the Room," *Bereavement Magazine, A Magazine of Hope and Healing* (Colorado Springs, Colo.), reprinted by permission; hereafter referred to by author's name and followed by *Bereavement*.

Session 5

1. Linda M. Lorenzo, "Definition," *Bereavement*.
2. Thelda Bevens, "On Being a Widow," used by permission.
3. Bobbi Graham, "First Time," used by permission.
4. Ellen Robbins, "My First Memorial Day," used by permission.
5. Nadine Smith, "If I Could Do It Over," used by permission.
6. Sybil Gibson, "Our Times Together," used by permission.
7. Alan D. Wolfelt, M. D., *Bereavement* (Feb. 1990), 34.
8. Wolfelt, *Bereavement* (March/April 1990), 34.

Session 6

1. Gail Brook Burket, "The Stepping-stone Prayer," on bookmark by *Guideposts*, (Carmel, N.Y.), used by permission of the author.
2. Helen Steiner Rice, "This Too Will Pass Away," used with permission of the Helen Steiner Rice Foundation.
3. Nan R. Kenton, MA, MC, "Surviving Holidays and Anniversaries," *Hospice of Bend Volunteer Manual*, used by permission.
4. Dave Williams, excerpt from "A Mother's Day Celebration," *Meditations*.
5. Judith O'Conner, "Do They Celebrate Christmas in Heaven?" used by permission.

6. Barbara Baumgardner, "A Christmas Gift for Me."

7. Sr. Teresa McIntier, CSI, RNm, MB, excerpts from "You'll Know You Are Recovering When:" *Hospice of Bend Grief Manual,* used by permission.

8. Barbara Baumgardner, "The Aroma of Recovery," *Meditations.*

Session 7

1. Martin Luther King Jr., Civil Rights March (Washington, D.C., Aug. 28,1963).

2. Author unknown, quoted in *Topical Encyclopedia of Living Quotations* (Minneapolis, Minn.: Bethany House Publishers), 26:339.

3. Excerpt reprinted from Og Mandino, *The Greatest Salesman in the World* (New York, N.Y.: Bantam Books, 1967 © by Og Mandino).

4. Darcie Sims, columnist, *Bereavement* (Nov./Dec 1990), 15.